S0-BNB-698

Paper Bag Prayers

Finding God in Little Things:
Any Time, Any Place

Bernadette McCarver Snyder

Liguori
LIGUORI, MISSOURI

Imprimi Potest:
Thomas D. Picton, C.Ss.R.
Provincial, Denver Province
The Redemptorists

Published by Liguori Publications
Liguori, Missouri
www.liguori.org

Library of Congress Cataloging-in-Publication Data

Snyder, Bernadette McCarver.
    Paper bag prayers : finding God in little things ; any time, any place / Bernadette McCarver Snyder.—1st ed.
        p. cm.
    ISBN 0-7648-1383-8
    1. Catholic women—Prayer-books and devotions—English. 2. Meditations. I. Title.
BX2170.W7S69   2006
242'.8—dc22   2005028348

Liguori Publications, a nonprofit corporation, is an apostolate of the Redemptorists. To learn more about the Redemptorists, visit *Redemptorists.com.*

Printed in the United States of America
10 09 08 07 06   5 4 3 2 1
First edition

Contents

Introduction

Busy, Busy? No Time to Look, Listen, or Pray? And What's a Paper Bag Prayer Anyway?

It's a to-go kind of prayer, fast food for thought, a lesson I learned that could fit right into any busy, hurry-up life—and I hope it will fit into yours too.

The idea is to choose any item small enough to fit into a paper bag—and then talk to God about it. Why? Well, it started a few years ago when I was trying to teach children about prayer. Occasionally, I would put little items into a lunch-size paper bag—a nickel, a shell, a sock, a key, and so on, and bring it to class. I would invite one child to reach into the bag and, without looking, choose one item. Whatever it was, we would talk about it and make up a prayer about it—thanking, praising, or asking God for help.

By focusing on one small everyday item at a time, I hoped this would show them how you can talk to God and pray about ANYthing, ANY place, ANY time. And it was amazing to see how this led us down so many different prayer paths.

As usual, in teaching, I learned—and found this fast, easy, private way to pray myself. Now I don't take a paper bag along with me everywhere, but when there's an "idle" moment—waiting, taking a coffee break, or doing some mindless task—I look around and focus on one small thing and am usually surprised at how it leads to a mini-meditation or a little conversation with God.

As you know, there is no "right" way to pray—all ways are good. We all know the beautiful "standard" prayers and have our own favorites. So at first, you may find it strange to be meditating on a shoelace or a postage stamp, but maybe it will help you find a new awareness, a new prayer direction.

The brief "to-go" conversations in this book are examples of my own paper bag prayers. With them, I invite you to look through the bits and pieces in the paper bag of your own daily life and pull out one item each day—and just talk to God about it.

And if you're too busy or just don't feel like packing a paper bag, reach into mine. Maybe you'll find some fast, easy-to-swallow, nourishing food-for-thought sandwiched together with a little laugh and a little prayer.

Dedication

To the faithful readers who have put up with my wandering way of writing, to all God's busy people everywhere who are sometimes a day late and a dollar short, and in gratitude to God who has filled my days with such strange, surprising, and serendipitous bits and pieces, detours and delights, laughter and lessons. My paper bag overfloweth—and I hope yours does too.

We are cups, constantly and quietly being filled.
The trick is, knowing how to tip ourselves over
and let the beautiful stuff out.

RAY BRADBURY

All Strung Out!

W hen I look at this ball of string, so many images come to mind.

I think of a bundle of newspapers tied with string to go in the recycling bin. I remember the lovely song that has the line, "...brown paper packages tied up with string...these are a few of my favorite things." But mostly, I think of a kite.

Dear Lord, it's so much fun watching a kite climbing the steps of the wind, wobbling at first, then taking off and confidently soaring higher and higher. Maybe kids love kites because they love the idea of flying. Maybe they like to run with a kite string so they feel attached to something that is actually touching the sky.

Lord, sometimes when you and I talk, I feel like I am running, clutching a string, soaring higher and higher, reaching for you, touching you.

But there are also those days when my kite gets stuck in a tree or fails to catch the wind and hits the dirt. And that's OK, Lord. I always know there's another time, another wind, another mysterious brown paper package of a day that I can shake and rattle and wonder what's inside before I open it and find what new adventures or insights or messages you have sent.

Thank you, Lord, for this ball of string and all of the possibilities it suggests. Thank you for reminding me that whether or not I'm being dutiful and recycling, whether I'm running or stumbling, whether I like what I find when I open the package each day, I can still rejoice as long as I hold onto that string that keeps me attached to you.

Pass the Paper Cup

How in the world did someone ever get the idea to make a cup out of paper! Whoever it was, I bet all of his or her friends laughed and made jokes about what a stupid idea it was. Imagine! Paper instead of china or glass or tin— paper strong enough to hold hot coffee or cold tea or maybe even soup. What a crazy idea.

And now, there are all kinds of paper cups—at home, at restaurants, at picnics, even at parties. And none of them have to be washed. What a crazy WONDERFUL idea!

Of course, Lord, I know we couldn't have paper cups if you hadn't made all those trees that can turn into paper that can turn into cups. Thanks, Lord. And Lord, forgive me for sometimes laughing at others who have new ideas that don't fit into my idea of how to do things properly.

Clamp my mouth shut and open my mind before I too quickly call something or someone silly or foolish. You and I know that I myself am one of the crazies who have had some weird ideas. Some of my friends laughed at me too, but you were one of the friends who didn't. Whenever I shared my ditzy ideas with you, I somehow knew that you would help me at least try to make them work; if they didn't work, I somehow knew that you would help me lift my chin off the floor and try again.

Lord, I guess you can understand your people when we try to "think out of the box," because lots of people laughed at you too with your crazy ideas about turning the other cheek and forgiving sinners and loving your neighbor as yourself.

Oh, Lord, it's so good to visit with you like this while I'm having my first morning cup of hot coffee. But gotta run now. It's time to refill this crazy paper cup!

Map It Out!

It's just a big piece of paper with lines and writing on it, but a map can sure come in handy when you're trying to find a place you've never been before. There's just one problem. If you have an old map like I sometimes do, some lines are left off and I'm left out in the great beyond wondering where to turn next.

It would be OK if one of my maps was old enough to be a treasure map, but, no, they're just old enough to get me lost. And even if they do get me where I'm going, the next step is trying to "rassle" them back into the neat fold where they started out.

Well, Lord, that's the story of my life. I set out to go somewhere or do something and I miss a turn or hit a detour and end up in a surprising situation. But that's OK, Lord, I know you have a strange sense of humor and you love to send me someplace I never meant to go, to do something I never meant to do. And yes, I have to admit that your travel plans always turn out to be MUCH more exciting than what I had mapped out.

So thanks, Lord, for being such a good travel agent and adding all these surprising stops and layovers and unexpected discoveries and unearned delights in my journey.

You've put a lot of mileage on me, Lord, but I've enjoyed every minute (well, almost every minute!).

Now, Lord, if you could just show me how to refold those maps!

Is It a Camel or an Apple Pie?

What did parents do before crayons were invented? All those bright colors in one little box—opening the door to imagination. All you need is one crayon and a piece of paper to get a child busy turning out a masterpiece while you're waiting in a restaurant for the grilled-cheese sandwich to arrive or sitting in church waiting for a song to end or trapped anywhere that you have to pass the time waiting.

And what about something to hang on the refrigerator door? What would you do without all those hand-drawn pictures of a school bus— or is it supposed to be a sunset or a camel or maybe an apple pie? And then there are those real treasures—the birthday or Mother's Day or Father's Day cards—made by hand with love and imagination and crayon.

Yes, Lord, crayons are a great blessing, but they also can teach us boring old grownups a lesson. Did you ever watch a kid with a crayon, hunched over a piece of paper, totally engrossed and focused on that drawing—a picture of undiluted concentration?

If only, Lord, we could learn that trick of undiluted concentration when we pray. Learned or rote prayers are wonderful and necessary. It's great to pray together as a family or a community, saying the same words that are familiar. But sometimes when you are "reciting" prayers you may have learned years ago, it's so easy for your mind to wander. Whether you're in church or driving a car or in a hospital waiting room or even sitting alone in a beautiful garden, when you're using memorized words to pray, it's easy to start thinking of what you need to do NEXT or what you forgot to do BEFORE or a million things that intrude in a busy brain.

So, Lord, help us—and especially me—to be reminded of that undiluted concentration of a child with a crayon. Help me realize what joy it can be to communicate with you, one on one, totally focused, tuning out all distractions, tuning in only you—having a little crayon prayer.

More Than a Coverup

My grandma and the ladies of her day made the most wonderful quilts. But all I have is this little quilted square that I use as a hot pad under a casserole.

Grandma's quilts were used as layers of coverups when houses didn't have very good central heating. They were also handy to put over a sleepy child taking a nap on the sofa or to spread on the grass under a tree for a picnic. And sometimes the fancy ones were memory quilts.

Those ladies saved every scrap of fabric from their own family and even beyond so each square brought back a memory from a favorite dress worn to a wedding or a special party or from a little girl's dress for the first day of school or a little boy's first pair of long pants. But a square might also come from Aunt Matilda's apron (she's the one who made that great four-layer jam cake) or Uncle George's Sunday shirt (he's the one who told so many corny jokes).

Well, Lord, the only memory my quilted hot pad will have is from which casserole tasted good and which one was the kind you'd try to erase from your culinary memory. But that's OK. It's pretty and useful. And it also makes me think of my grandmother and her quilts and causes me to mull over the memory of some of those family members who were saints or sinners, sweet or sour, kooks or characters. Thank you, Lord, for the gift of memory. Help me to learn from the mistakes of the past, revel in the joyful successes, and laugh at both the good and the not-so-good.

In today's fast-moving technological world, the only kind of "time travel" yet discovered is that of memory. And as I travel back, Lord, you are there in every square, a loving coverup for the fabric of my life and my family.

Looky, Looky!

What a funny name—a kaleidoscope. But what a fun, magical invention. When I hold it up to my eye and looky, looky, the little colored bits of glass jiggle and joggle as I turn the tube so I can enjoy a rainbow of designs and patterns and maybe daydreams.

The kaleidoscope makes me daydream about the patterns in my life and how they also change from day to day and sometimes from moment to moment. Some days are filled with appointments, meetings, duties. Some are taken up with shopping, cooking, gardening. And some are well-planned until the phone rings and in a moment, the schedule changes to make room for a small emergency or an invitation or maybe even an adventure.

Thank you, Lord, for this kaleidoscopic life. When I sit in a restaurant or a waiting room or ride on an airport shuttle bus, Lord, I often look at all the other people around who are "with me" but apart. I know they each lead a life that may be similar or totally different from mine. They may come from disparate worlds, have had experiences I can't imagine, have read books or learned languages or traveled in circles or cities that are totally unknown to me. And they surely have different daydreams than mine. But we are all eating, waiting, riding together—yet alone.

Sometimes, Lord, I start judging those "others" by their looks or mannerisms. Sometimes I see a face that triggers fear or envy or giggles or nosy curiosity. And then I remember that you made them all, Lord. You know them all. You gave them each a kaleidoscope too, distinct from mine. You also allowed them the freedom to jiggle and joggle their days to make their own patterns and designs just as I do. I guess some are more limited in the choices available and some just think they are more limited because they get stuck on one pattern or design and are afraid to change it.

Thank you, Lord, for kaleidoscopes and for free will. And thank you for all those "others" who make this journey so interesting.

Smile...

The toothless grin of a first-grader, the radiant smile of a bride peeking over her bouquet, two little girls caught in a giggle, two teenage boys snickering over a secret joke. What stories a little snapshot can suggest.

Usually I have a snap or two of my grandson tucked in my purse for instant joy, but I have a bookcase lined with albums for an afternoon of memory. My mother's album alone is good for an hour, poring over black-and-white scenes showing ancestors I never knew or barely remember. Oh, their clothes, their hairdos, their poses—what were they thinking? And then there are some of my own albums showing me and my friends living the modern life. Oh, those clothes, those hairdos, those poses—what were we thinking?

Dear Lord, times change, but maybe people don't change as much as we expect or suspect. What do you think, Lord? Are your people of today worse or better than those of another day and time? Have we learned from the experiences of earlier generations to be smarter or kinder or more loving or more religious? Or have we become greedy, selfish, thoughtless, immoral, and irreligious? Are we less or more or just about the same?

Well, Lord, I guess you are the wrong one to ask such a question. Unlike us, you don't have to carry around snapshots or thumb through albums from the past. You see all, know all, and judge all. You know we sometimes behave stupidly or wickedly and disappoint you. In fairness, you judge and ask us to repent. But you know us by heart and love all your children— past, present, and future.

Help us, Lord, to be worthy of that love. And show me, Lord, how to live so that I won't be so embarrassed when I look back at my life's snapshots. Teach me to not just pose for the camera but to be truly the person you would like to see in the photo so that when I hold up my life to you and say, "Smile..." you will!

Play It Safe

It's just a piece of twisted metal and it doesn't get much respect today— but the safety pin must have been a wham-bang idea when it first appeared. It must have revolutionized baby diapering and saved the day for anyone who had a button pop off at an embarrassing moment. It must have been used millions of times to pin a note to a teacher on a child's blouse or jacket. And it became a staple in sewing kits, travel kits, and maybe even first-aid kits.

Since then, we have zippers, Velcro, and no-pin diapers, but when the safety pin was first invented, it must have seemed almost like a miracle.

Lord, this little pin made me think about miracles today. Just in this century, we've had so many miracles—planes that let people actually fly through the air, microwave ovens that magically heat food without fire, and such technological impossibilities as television, computers, audio and videotapes, DVDs, cell phones, and an endless selection of unimaginables in every store. All these are "miracles" we take for granted now.

Of course, the real miracles come from you, Lord—just as all the ideas for our worldly miracles came from the imagination you gave to the inventors. But today, Lord, I want you to know how grateful I am for my own little miracles. Every morning I wake up and think how lucky I am to have a cozy bed to sleep in every night, a comfortable home where I feel safe, a tiny garden full of flowers and bees and birds in the trees, an old but trusty car in the garage that can take me to interesting places where I sometimes meet amazing people—and this is just the beginning of my thank-you list.

You know I'm grateful for my family and friends and the microwave oven and my computer are great, but today I thank you for the little daily miracles that are so easy to take for granted. Thank you for books to read and music to cheer me and hot tea to warm my heart's cockles and iced drinks to soothe my fevered brow. And thanks for this little safety pin that always travels with me in my purse, just in case I need it to save me in a sticky situation.

Yummy, Yummy!

Happiness is a warm cookie! Well, it is to some of us. When the day turns sour and you need a pickup, sometimes a sweet and warm—or even a cold and kinda stale—cookie just hits the spot. At least, it works for me!

That's why it's not hard to meditate on a cookie. It leads easily to the three forms of prayer: praising you, Lord, for inspiring someone to come up with the idea of turning flour, sugar, and some odds and ends into yummies for the tummy; thanking you, Lord, for planting sugar cane in our earthly habitat so we could figure out how to use it to sweeten our lives; and asking you, Lord, to forgive me for sometimes enjoying your sweet gifts a little too much.

But, Lord, that's just the beginning. There are so many types of cookies that could provide food for thought. A chocolate chip can spur me to start chipping away at my to-do chore list but also to take another look at my to-wish list of goals and get to work again on my impossible or maybe possible dreams.

A lemon-drop cookie reminds me to say thanks for all the times the things or people I thought were lemons in my life turned out to be sweet lemonade. And any kind of sugar cookie brings back memories of the ones my mother used to roll out on the kitchen counter and the ones I used to put in my son's lunch bag and the ones a friend brought in to sweeten my recovery when I was really sick.

And, Lord, I mustn't forget all the fortune cookies I have opened to read the predictions that I will be healthy, wealthy, and wise; find romance and adventure in my life; and some day learn to look before I leap. Thank you, Lord, that some of those predictions came true—but I'm still waiting for the wealthy and wise.

But, Lord, the best cookie inspiration is to meditate on all the other sweet things in life— like the people I know, love, or just encounter along the way who give me joy, thoughtfulness, kindness, helpfulness, and surprises too! Thanks, Lord, for making life such a chocolate-chip, lemon-drop, sugar-frosted, unpredictable banquet.

Hear, Hear!

This little seashell is too small for me to hold to my ear and expect to hear the ocean— but if I use my imagination, maybe I can!

Oh yes, I can hear the ocean's waves crashing on the rocks just like I did that day in California when I was so happily engrossed in the sea and the sun and the book I was reading that I didn't notice the cute little field mouse who was busily chewing through my lunch sack, planning to share my sandwich—which he did.

But wait, I can also hear the gentle swirling sound of the pool in the Japanese garden where I first saw those brilliantly colored Coy fish. And yes, yes, I can hear the sound of the dishwasher ending its cycle, reminding me it is almost time to put away the clean dishes, cook supper, and refill it with dirty dishes. Ah...the cycle of my life.

Lord, every time I find a serene moment to ponder a seashell or listen to the birds chirping from the birdhouse or the wind rustling the leaves in the trees or the whispering of happy memories, it's time to stop and return to reality.

Well, maybe that's because I don't allow enough downtime so I won't have to hurry through serenity, just like I don't always allow enough time to listen for your voice. Maybe you've been trying to get my attention, hoping to send a message I really need to hear. Maybe you've been trying to show me the solution to a problem I've been worrying about or to tell me how to find acceptance and appreciation of a person or a chore or a silly little snag that has been driving me up the wall with irritation and frustration.

Or maybe, Lord, you were just trying to contact me to assure me of your presence and protection—and patience.

Thank you, Lord, for seashells and ocean waves, for field mice and Coy fish, for bird sounds and breezes. And yes, Lord, thank you also for electric dishwashers and the realities of my life and your love.

Packet of Possibilities!

The picture on the front is pretty but when you open a flower-seed packet and look inside, it takes a lot of faith to think those ugly little seeds will some day turn into a beautiful bouquet of flowers like the ones on the front of the packet. And yet, if you plant properly, watch and water carefully, they very often do. Not always, but very often.

And that's life. Whether it's a new idea or a hope or a goal or a child, you gotta plant it properly and watch it very carefully and keep watering it and feeding it correctly or it just won't grow into what you were expecting. It seems like it takes such a long time, you almost give up the dream—but the operative word is faith. You gotta have faith.

And sometimes, even after you've had faith, you realize that it's not gonna happen. A drought comes and kills your garden. Your great idea or hope or goal doesn't work out. Your kids grow in a direction you never expected. But,

Lord, that's when you gotta have REAL faith. That's when you have to give up the dream of the beautiful bouquet like the picture on the packet…and somehow manage to accept and say, "God's will be done."

Yes, Lord, I know YOU already know all that and even I know all that in my head, but sometimes an ugly little weed seed sprouts up and I want to get mad at you and tell you my idea was better than yours. I want to remind you that I kept my end of the bargain and watched and worked and even sacrificed a big part of my life to make that dream come true, but you didn't make it happen. I want to say, "What's the matter with you, Lord, weren't you paying attention?"

Actually, Lord, you know that I didn't just WANT to say all those things. I really said them to you, didn't I? And still you didn't send a bolt of lightning to smite me and you didn't stop being my friend. That's why, Lord, I keep planting those ugly little seeds, keep believing in the picture on the packet, and keep knowing that some day you and I will stand in a beautiful garden together.

Spoon It Up!

Pass the pudding, pass the potatoes, pass the soup, and spaghetti sauce. What would we do without spoons—both small and large? We start out with those tiny baby spoons. Some are silver and some are shaped like an airplane and some are just little spoons that deliver pudding and smashed carrots and awful green puréed spinach. Then we move on to pots of homemade soup and big bowls of mashed potatoes and spaghetti and then we need really big spoons so a hungry family can share.

Lord, just the word *spoon* can stir up a variety of memories: a baby spoon with tooth marks on it, days when sweethearts would "spoon" by the light of the silvery moon, or the friend with a gift of gab who sometimes "spoons it on too thickly."

And then there's the memory I have of a crotchety uncle who outlived his wife and alienated most friends and family, then left a will telling the executor to divide his property evenly between two charities—except for one silver tablespoon. That was to be sent to some lady in Keokuk. We never knew if the executor found the lady or if she knew why she was receiving a spoon, but it sure caused a lot of family conversation and speculation.

Lord, as I'm stirring the sugar into my orange tea today, I think the lesson of a spoon is the idea of dependence and independence. As babies, we are totally dependent. Then we move into those teen years when we want to be "totally independent." Finally, we settle into adulthood where we realize how much we must depend on such things as clean air and water, the whims of bosses, and oh my!—electricity. If we ever doubt our dependence, just wait until there's a blackout and we can't read or watch TV or use the computer and we can't even escape the darkness because the garage door won't open until the electricity comes back on.

Yes, Lord, I know there are even more important things we depend on like the love and support of others and always, ultimately, we must depend on you and your love for us. Thank you, Lord, for letting me depend on you and bend your ear with all my triumphs and tragedies. And, Lord, forgive me if I'm one of those friends who sometimes spoons it on too thickly.

Day by Day...

My days are numbered. They're all here on this little pocket calendar. It tells me where and when I'm supposed to go every day. It just doesn't always tell me what I'm supposed to do when I get there. Sometimes it tells me I'm supposed to go to a meeting or a luncheon or a friend's house or a doctor's office or church, and so on. Sometimes it reminds me I better stay home and get some work done. But once I reach my appointed location, I'm on my own.

That's when you come in, Lord. You're supposed to tell me when to keep my mouth shut or speak out at a meeting, when to react "properly" to whoever is seated next to me at the luncheon, when to not stay too long or leave too soon at my friend's house. Well, Lord, sometimes you must forget or you're just insisting on that free-will business and that's when I get into trouble.

At the meeting, I open mouth and insert foot. At the luncheon, I take an immediate dislike to my lunch buddy and neglect to put on a happy face when that person might really need some friendly conversation. And even when I stay home, I start straightening but stop to read a newspaper or book that got left under a chair or

I start cleaning the kitchen but stop for one snack too many.

Well, again, why am I telling you all this, Lord? You've seen me in action. Forgive me, Lord. You have been so generous to give me all those wonderful days, some better than others—but each full of possibilities and opportunities. Teach me to know when I should do more and when I should do less. Give me the wisdom to use your time wisely and stop frittering away all those numbered days in my pocket calendar.

It's So Tacky!

What's so good about a thumbtack? It's sharp and pointy. It's hard to hold and easy to drop. And if you drop it on the floor, it's so little, it's hard to find. But if you don't find it and step on it, it can give you a big ouchie. However! A thumbtack is great for putting notes on a bulletin board, sticking posters on a wall, or even hanging up a lightweight picture when you don't want to hammer a nail into the wall. Yep, even a little thumbtack is nothing to thumb your nose at!

Dear Lord, I would never call a useful, helpful thumbtack tacky, but I'm afraid I have been guilty of calling some things and some people tacky. I know, I know, Lord, I am too quick to criticize. I know one person's tacky is another's treasure. And besides, who am I to judge?

Lord, I know you are the only one to judge things more important than tacky, but today's society tells us it is NEVER nice to be judgemental. And yes, that is important. But, Lord, it is so easy to go too far with that mental suggestion. It can lead us to look at someone doing something that is obviously sinful, immoral, hurtful, hateful, illegal, illicit, or just plain mean, and by our silence seem to accept it and even condone it.

One day, we left the door ajar and a little naughtiness crept in and opened it wider and now we are drowning in a culture that is beyond tacky. Yet we look at the trash and say tsk, tsk instead of NO, NO. We politely tolerate it in order to not be judgmental.

You must be so disappointed with us, Lord, wondering when we are going to open our eyes and our mouths and speak up, speak out, complain, and object about this trashy way of life. Help us, Lord, to see the difference between nonjudgmental and godless. Help us, Lord, to get the point so we can start to thumb our noses at this worse-than-tacky world.

It's Not Easy Being Green!

A little green leaf does not take up much space in a paper bag or in a life. But there is magic in this leaf. It may play a small part, but it does play a part in making a tree, a park, a forest. And looking at it can conjure up different ideas for different people.

A little boy might look at a leaf and think of a tree to climb. A botanist might look at it and say, "photosynthesis." A young girl could look at it and visualize a sunny springtime day and a leafy tree where she could sit and read a favorite book. And perhaps, someone of any age could look at it and think of a park, a forest, or a backyard that provides sanctuary.

Ah yes, Lord, this tiny green leaf can be magic. I look at it and think of lots of things—the backyard tree my son liked to climb, the day in school when I first heard about the miracle of photosynthesis, the times I played hooky from chores to read a book under a shady tree, and the days I sought sanctuary in nature to change a blue mood into a fresh new green insight, or to just praise you for giving the world so much beauty.

Only you, Lord, could put so much food for thought in a tiny green leaf. Actually, Lord, this leaf also brings to mind other leaves in my life: parsley, basil, rosemary, and thyme—the spices I like to use in the kitchen. And then there are the leaves of my photo albums, recalling the "days of our lives" and bringing a smile or a tear.

Lord, you made so many large spectacular things in this world—mountains, oceans, rainbows—but I'm glad you put magic into the small ones too. This leaf reminds me of my smallness and the smallness of all us ordinary folk. It also challenges me to remember that we small ones can also be magic if we use the life you gave us to climb, notice miracles, read to keep learning, and seek sanctuary with you.

What's Cooking?

This recipe card is one of my most valued possessions, but I didn't realize it until recently. I read an article about people who had been forced to evacuate their homes with little warning—because of flood, fire, tornado, and so on. They all told what treasured possessions they chose to grab and save.

A smart lady grabbed her purse that held the cards she needed for identification—driver's license, insurance, and so forth. Others saved family photos, a favorite heirloom, jewelry, or clothing. But one lady said she saved her recipe file. I would never have thought of that, but it made me realize how much I treasure my well-thumbed, smudged, and scribbled-on recipe cards.

Lord, I know this must sound trivial, but some of those cards have my mother's handwriting on them and they call to mind all the delicious goodies she turned out for her ladies' luncheons and our family get-togethers plus the "standards" she made for everyday meals.

And then there are my own treasured recipes for special occasions or family favorites. I have some memorized but when I'm cooking for company, I still check the recipe card to be sure I'm not leaving out a half-teaspoon of something.

Funny, isn't it, Lord, how a little three-by-five card can bring back so many memories? And isn't it funny how certain foods recall happy times? I guess you can understand that, Lord, since I notice in the Bible that you too were often sharing a meal with your apostles or being invited to go to someone's home for dinner. Maybe this should tell me that I better start spending more time with the Bible than with my recipe cards. But, Lord, the Bible is so much longer and harder to read than those little three-by-fives.

Thank you, Lord, for all the happy times with food and fun. And thank you for the Bible and all the lessons to be learned and all the memories of your sacrifice and love for your worldwide family. And, Lord, I promise to get out of the kitchen and into the Bible more frequently.

All Hail the Snail

I do love e-mail, but this little postage stamp reminds me that for years—through rain, snow, sleet, or hail—the "snail mail" has arrived daily at my mailbox in the front yard. And how I love to get a handful of envelopes out of the box, even if most of them hold bills or advertising. Ever hopeful, I thumb through, looking for a REAL letter in there somewhere.

They come a lot less frequently now, but sometimes there is a real letter or a check or a crayoned drawing—all treasures. The e-mail doesn't have to go through snow or sleet, but it travels through lots of channels and wires and can so easily be erased. A letter can live for generations, but an e-mail usually lasts only a few minutes.

Well, Lord, that's progress for you. Soon no one will find a trove of letters, carefully saved and tied with blue ribbons. There may be a few floppies or CDs saved, but the messages on them will be irretrievable because the computers they were made on will have long since become obsolete. I hate to think of all those lost memories, but I realize that sometimes we waste today by spending too much time thinking of yesterdays.

Opening envelopes of the past and pining over what could have or might have been can take away the joy of what is. Today may not be perfect but it's the only reality, the only time that can be changed or improved. So, Lord, let this little postage stamp teach me to be grateful for the many happy memories of the past and show me how to stop dwelling on the unhappy ones by turning them over to you, to forgive and erase.

Lord, let me live in the present so I can relish and use each today wisely. Show me how to enjoy as many minutes as possible, then use any painful minutes as lessons to be learned and steps to grow on. Then maybe—through snow and sleet, computer glitches and lost e-mails, I will be worthy to earn your stamp of approval!

Cotton on a Stick?

What an unusual idea—
a little stick with a dab
of cotton on the tip of it! Yet
you'll find these in most home
medicine cabinets and many first-
aid kits. In fact, it's so popular that
almost everybody has needed and used
one at some time or another. Sooo, this
little swab makes me realize that just
because something is little and unimportant
looking, it can still do some very important
jobs. In fact, it can do some jobs just because it
IS little.

These cotton-on-a-sticks are great for cleanup
jobs on delicate babies and not-so-delicate
adults. They're good for reaching into small
places and even dusting places that only
something that small could reach.

Dear Lord, when I see one of these, let that
tell me that I should also have proper respect for
people who may be unimportant looking or who
may do non-executive but very important jobs
like visiting the sick, working in a soup kitchen
or food pantry, giving rides to elderly non-
drivers, caring for a disabled child, cleaning
other people's houses, taking casseroles and hugs
to the bereaved.

Actually, Lord, I DO respect them. In fact, I am in awe of them. They are the people who put big smiles into our everyday world.

And Lord, those smiles make me think of another kind of cotton-on-a-stick. I first saw it at a county fair when I was a little girl and I've loved it ever since—pink cotton candy, a small treat that has brought big smiles to kids of all ages.

Thank you, Lord, for whoever thought of putting a dab of cotton on a little stick and cottony candy on a bigger one. And thanks for all those wonderful "small" people—often unnoticed, often unseen—who serve us, and serve you, so well every day.

Play Ball

W hen I look at this little ball, it makes me feel happy and bouncy! Maybe that's why someone coined the phrase, "Have a ball!"

A baseball, a football, or a golf ball all remind you of a game, a fun time—and that magic word *play*. And this little round red ball came with an old-time game called "jacks" that must be new again because I just found a set in the toy department.

Today, when there are cell phones and iPods® and video games to be played, playing a game of "jacks" sounds like ancient history. But simple games like that plus board games and guessing games and just running through the sprinkler in the summer or using your imagination to make up your own games in the winter probably caused more giggles and fun than playing today's beeping electronic computerized games.

Unfortunately, today some people seem to think that even the word *play* is ancient history—one of those unmentionable four-letter words. Another four-letter word, *work*, has become the magic one. Many have decided that work should be a 24-7 occupation in order to get a bigger house, bigger car, bigger title, and all the perks of "success." Maybe these are all worthy goals, but not if work leaves no time for play.

Lord, thank you for all the wonderful times in my life when I found time to play and for all the times when I have been fortunate to have profitable and enjoyable work. Help me, and help all today's busy bees, to learn how to find a happy medium between the two, spending the proper amount of time on each—plus enough time left over to pray!

If we could just manage to do that, Lord, then every day we could have a ball!

I Carrot a Lot

Why is it that carrots look so good, with their cheery orange color and fancy fringy greenery—until you're on a diet. Then they just look low calorie, which is seldom fun. Personally, I like my carrots drenched in butter and a bit of maple syrup or orange marmalade so I carrot a lot at suppertime. But, in my continuing interest in trivia, I just discovered a new carrot claim.

The trivia fact simply stated that carrots were not orange until the sixteenth century. So what color were they? And why did they turn orange? Mine is not to question why...mine is just to wonder why because I have no idea where to look for the rest of that intriguing information.

Well, Lord, that's one of today's many unique problems. We are constantly exposed to "sound bites"—not just in trivia bits but in overheard conversations at the grocery or as a result of interrupted conversations at meetings or especially on the supposedly factual network news programs. We hear a tidbit that catches our ears and we want to know more about it but we seldom get the full story (unless it's a shocking story of a celebrity and then we hear MORE than the full story).

So here I am, Lord, living in a society where we are constantly tempted to judge without all the facts, gathering opinions based on just a bit of trivia or a dab of news or clues or slanted views. Help me, Lord, to be more careful about making snap decisions when I have too little information. Teach me to look further and reach wider before I get all riled up and suddenly turn orange like that sixteenth-century carrot!

Lord, I'm afraid I sometimes do that with your teachings too. I might hear some "important" person's opinion on TV and it sounds so good, I might quickly agree without digging a bit deeper to make up my own opinion, based on your word and your way. Lord, I know you are the only important one I should listen to but sometimes I get carried away and led astray.

Help me, Lord, to be wary of sound bites. And Lord, if you know how I can find out why those carrots turned orange, please lead me to the proper carrot family tree so I can get my facts straight.

Buttoned Up

This slightly battered button just fell off my raincoat. Guess it got tired of being out in the rain, snow, and dark of night and has gone on strike. It will probably get a good rest since there will be a lot of procrastination before I get around to sewing it back on. But it does make me think of all the kinds of buttons in my world.

There's the button that rings the doorbell, signaling me to welcome friends...the buttons (or switches) that turn on the lights, the coffee pot, the vacuum cleaner, the microwave oven, and so on. Then there's the garage-opener button that frees me and my car to explore the world outside, and of course, the button on the computer that connects me to the wide, wide world of the Internet.

My goodness, Lord, without all those buttons, I could be sitting in the dark—hungry, cold, alone, friendless, coffee-less, and not computerized. Well, not really, Lord. With the help of some knowledgeable technicians, I'd find a way to get out, back in, and logged on. But thank you, Lord, for all those buttons that make my life work the way it does.

And, Lord, let's not discuss the way some people manage to "push my buttons" and irritate me until I do not respond the way a good Christian should. And let's overlook those days when I get so buttoned up, I can't see the forest for the trees or see another person's viewpoints since my own are filling my brain and restricting my view of the big picture.

Lord, I guess those are the times when I push YOUR buttons and you must wonder why I can't always act and react in a way that would reflect your teachings. Well, Lord, I guess I'm like that raincoat button. Sometimes I just forget to hang on and I let go.

That's when I'm glad, Lord, that you don't procrastinate like I do. You don't take too long to get me sewn back into my proper place. Thank you for always finding me when I fall or get lost. Thank you for getting me reattached quickly so I am once again ready to face the rain, the snow, the dark of night—and the vacuum cleaner, the computer....

Number, Please!

What's this? A little card with instructions about how to teach children when and how to "Call 911." Oh, yes, this is an easy number to remember and an important one.

Once upon a time, before cell phones, before dial phones, waaay back, when you picked up a phone, an operator would come on the line and say, "Number, please." You could talk to the operator and request the number of the person you wanted to reach. Now you just punch in a number and, hopefully, your call will go through automatically.

Today I was thinking about that, Lord, when I heard a siren in the distance that probably meant someone had called 911 and the emergency call was being answered. When I was in elementary school, a teacher told us that whenever we heard a siren, we should say a little prayer for whoever was in an emergency situation at that time. I've never forgotten that. So I did that today. I do it every time I hear a siren. And, Lord, every time I have a personal emergency, I call YOU. The only problem, Lord, is that an operator does not answer and say, "Number, please." I know you've got my number, but I sometimes wonder if I've got yours.

Have I been sending so many 911 calls to you that they've piled up in your in-box? Lord, Lord, I'm just in a silly mood today. I know you hear my prayers and answer them. I've received my share of "no" answers, but I've got a lot of "yes" ones too. Thank you, Lord. Thank you for keeping me in your address book and I promise I will always keep you in mine.

Around and Around We Spin

I t's an old toy. It's a simple toy. But kids still love to watch a top spinning around and around. Where will it spin? When will it stop?

Maybe kids like tops because kids like to spin too. They like merry-go-rounds, ring-around-the-rosey, and just chasing one another around a tree. Well, sometimes I too can identify with a top, as I spin from chore to chore, multitasking, going around in circles—never the right circles! Where will I spin next? When, oh, when can I stop?

Lord, when you see me spinning, remind me of the whirling dervishes. Maybe they got the idea from watching kids run around a tree, because they whirl around and around an area, singing or chanting as they whirl. But this is their way of praying!

As the dervishes whirl and pray, they extend the right hand, facing up toward heaven and the left hand facing down, toward earth. They are praying to receive God's mercy in the right hand

and release it with the left, passing it on to the others on earth.

So why am I telling you this, Lord, since you already know all that? I am telling you because I want you to help me pray while I twirl. As you know, lots of us in my little corner of earth have too much of everything—except time. That's why we've gotten in the habit of doing two or three things at the same time. That's why we are in serious danger of spinning out of control!

Help us all, Lord, to start to do our daily skirmish like a dervish, to put a new spin on the idea of "pray always." Maybe this will even teach us, or at least teach me, to slow down my worldly whirl and start to go around in the right circle—yours.

Mirror, Mirror...

At the bottom of a drawer, I came across this little pocket-sized mirror that was a long-ago Christmas gift. It is so fancy, it's in a silver case and that's in a black velvet envelope. Unfortunately, when I looked into this fancy mirror, I saw that same old face I see in my ordinary mirror.

Oh well, mirrors are the good news-bad news story. Most mornings, I look into my bathroom mirror and think *what the heck happened here*? But occasionally, before I leave for a meeting or luncheon, I check with the mirror in the hall (where the lighting is very bad) and if I got a good night's sleep and I'm having a good hair day, I think *hmm...well, it could be worse*.

But no matter what my mirror tells me, I sometimes wonder how I really look to other people. Just suppose I got kidnapped and my relatives and friends had to go to a police sketch artist, how would they describe my face? I wonder if they would get it right. I wonder if anyone could look at that sketch and recognize me when they saw me in the kidnappers' clutches.

Well, Lord, I guess you are the only one who really knows what I look like. Do I look kind and generous and ever-loving and always open to new ideas? Or do I look hurried and harried, stingy with my time and possessions, loving only when it's convenient and stuck in a rut, glued to old ideas and old ways? Hmm...I guess the mirror, mirror on the wall doesn't know the real story after all—and maybe neither do I!

A face is just a face. No one but you, Lord, knows what lies behind that façade. Who am I, deep down, Lord? Am I really who I think I am or am I hiding behind a false face? Help me, Lord, to be who and what you want me to be so when those kidnappers strike, someone will be able to describe me accurately. And, Lord, I sure hope that police artist makes me look better than the sketches they show on those TV police shows.

Uh-oh, see how vain I am, Lord—hoping to look good even on a wanted poster!

Sew It Up!

It's just a spool of thread—a really tiny spool of thread. But to me, this is a treasure of great price. It fits into a small plastic bag full of other tiny spools of thread in every color of the rainbow. When I discovered this little bag in a store one day, I said to myself, *Aha...now this is my idea of "sewing supplies."* Each little spool has just enough thread for me to sew on a couple of buttons or repair a tiny tear. And that's my limit when it comes to sewing up something.

My mother's sewing machine sits in my basement, never-to-be-used again. It hates me. I gave up on it because it kept gnarling its threads, rejecting its bobbin, and making strange ugly noises every time I came near it. So now I'm happy with my little spools of thread and a roll of clear tape for emergency repair of a ripped hem.

The other day I heard you only need two tools in life...WD40 to get things to go and duct tape to get things to stay. Well, I have both of those PLUS my little spools of thread so I should be prepared for any emergency.

But of course, I'm not, Lord. I'm never prepared. I think I've got it all together and suddenly, one of the threads of my life starts to unravel and I go into panic mode. And there are so MANY threads—at home, work, church, clubs, and so on. I love them all, but it's very hard to keep them all untangled. I could never do it without you, Lord.

When I call for repairmen to come fix a problem, they say they can come a week from Tuesday, but I have to stay home from one to six because who knows what time they will arrive. When I call you, Lord, for help in repairing my rips and tears, sometimes I think you are like those repairmen. I never know when you will show up to help. But I have faith that, sooner or later, Lord, you WILL. You will, won't you? I have faith.

Forever Blowing Bubbles

This small bar of hand soap looks pretty bedraggled, especially since its wrapper got torn when it traveled home in my suitcase from a recent convention—but oh, it smells so good, like a lovely bouquet of flowers. And if I use it to scrub away potting soil under the fingernails, smudges of yellow mustard, or red tomato sauce stains, I know it will replace them with that lovely aroma!

Lord, I am so grateful I don't have to concoct homemade soap like the pioneer ladies did. I'm grateful for scented bar soap, liquid dishwashing soap, powdered laundry soap, and, oh yes, bubble bath.

But Lord, have you noticed how strange it is that those bubble-bath sprinkles come in all colors, yet once they foam up in the water, the bubbles are still white? Life is so full of mysteries like that. No wonder life is such fun.

Well, Lord, I hope my soap bouquet will remind me to wash out all the negative thoughts from my mind and inspire me to clean up, fix up, paint up, and do all the repairs that need to be done in my house and in my heart. And while I'm doing all that, Lord, please help me to not get into a lather about it all, because that will make those negative thoughts sneak back and then I will have to wash my hands of the whole idea and go eat a candy bar.

But, Lord, I just had a better idea. Since I am supposed to be meditating on this little bar of soap with its heavenly aroma, I was reminded of that fancy soap-bubble jar I was given as a favor at a party last week. Before I start on all this cleanup work, Lord, what would you think if I got out that little jar and took it out in the backyard? I know what the neighbors would think, but what would you think, Lord? I could open the jar, take out the bubble ring and just spend a silly time-out blowing bubbles, pretty bubbles in the air. "My, how they fly...nearly reach the sky...."

I'll send some prayers with them so watch, Lord, and you may see some happy bubbles reaching for your sky!

Pull Down the "Shades"

Good morning, Sunshine. You brighten my day and my way. But sometimes your light is so bright, I need these sunglasses so I can see where I'm going. And besides, maybe jazzy sunglasses will make me look like a movie star. Or maybe not.

Oh well, Lord, I long ago gave up trying to look like a movie star. But I haven't given up the habit of looking out each morning, hoping to see the golden glow of your sunlight instead of the drab gray of your rain. I know we need both and I thank you for both. But I'm always happy when I have to take along sunglasses. Wearing shades, I can be mysterious. I can hide. I can pretend to be somebody else, somebody more put-together.

And yes, Lord, I know that sometimes I do that even without the sunglasses. I pull down the shades so I won't have to see what I'm trying to avoid (like that messy basement). Sometimes I put on dark glasses because I am in a dark mood and I don't want to see the bright side of the day's problems. I don't want to think that the sun will come out tomorrow. I want to enjoy being miserable today.

And sometimes I don't want to see too clearly because I might have to face my own prejudice or lack of charity or plain old laziness. But enough about me. We were supposed to be talking about sunglasses today.

I remember, Lord, when it was cool to get as hot as possible so you could have a suntan to wear with your sunglasses. And of course I had cat-eye sunglasses decorated with rhinestones! Thank goodness, styles change. And thank goodness you DON'T, Lord. You're there turning on the sun and the moon every day. And you're always showing me new wonders to discover in your world, whether or not I'm wearing my shades!

It's a Puzzle!

I cut the crossword puzzle out of today's newspaper and put it in my purse so I'd have something to work on if I got stuck "waiting" somewhere. I love crossword puzzles, but sometimes they can be tricky. I can fly through one, penciling in answers as fast as I can write—until—I hit a clue that takes pondering. In the English language, one word can have so many different meanings. How about the word *entertain*? You can entertain an idea, entertain by playing the violin with a symphony, or just have a few friends in for dinner! And then there's the clue "cake topper." I immediately think of bride and groom or birthday candles, but no, the answer is "icing."

Of course, I know, Lord, the real puzzle is your wide and wonderful universe—and how to find my proper spot in it. I guess everyone wonders and ponders about that. Am I fulfilling my reason for being on earth? Do I have a mission? Have I missed the boat that would have taken me where I should have been?

It's so easy to indulge in "if only...." But when I mull over the past, I wonder if life really would have been better "if only." Were some of my decisions really bad choices, opportunities missed, wrong paths taken? Or were you there, leading me, helping me decide, sending me in a direction I needed to take to get where you wanted me to be?

Yes, Lord, I know that's the real answer. No matter how much I protested when I didn't get what I wanted, I am so grateful that you saw to it that instead I got what I needed.

But, Lord, you know that you are the greatest puzzle of all. No matter how much your children wonder and ponder, we can never figure out all your mysteries or discover all your secrets or figure out why you made us the way we are or sent us where we are. And that's what makes life great. You knew, didn't you, Lord, that it would be boring if we knew all the answers and could see around all the corners.

Now, since I can't solve all your puzzles, Lord, I'm gonna take a break and work on this crossword puzzle. Let's see...the nine-down clue is, "One who meanders." Does that remind you of anyone, Lord?

Yes, We Have No Bananas!

Delicious food, good for you, comes prepackaged in a bright shiny yellow easy-to-open package. Who could ask for anything more? Banana on your breakfast cereal, banana as a snack, banana to go in a pudding or a pie or a lunch sack or in your pocket. Now who ever thought of creating such a great food. Who else?

Dear Lord, thank you for giving us bananas. I love 'em. And Lord, as I was munching on one today I remembered that line from an old country music song, "Peel me a nanner, toss me a peanut; you sure made a monkey out of me." Well, Lord, as you know, I don't need any help making a monkey out of myself. Just yesterday I wrinkled my nose and made a terrible face when I was served some food I was sure I would NOT like—but then I did like it. Mugged like a monkey too soon.

Just last week, instead of swinging from a tree, I swung the car out of my driveway too fast and demolished my favorite garbage can. Showing off like a monkey instead of being careful. And oh, so many times I have shown my teeth and screeched and chattered about something that happened that seemed so earth-shakingly bad, so day-destroyingly miserable, so unrecoverably unfair. And then it all worked out just fine and I was embarrassed by my monkey shines.

Well, Lord, I must stop monkeying around with all these explanations. You know—and you forgive. But I just started out to tell you how much I like those yellow nanners. You thought of so many practical, necessary things for our planet—fresh water to drink, sunshine for light, dirt for gardens—but you also found time to give us beautiful things to look at and delicious things to eat. And then you gave us something that combines practical, beautiful, and delicious. Yes, we have some bananas—and thank you, thank you, thank you!

You Light Up My...

On the candle shelf in my pantry, I have one for every occasion—tea lights, vigil lights, short-fat, tall-elegant, once-lit, never-lit, pretty ones, ugly ones for emergency nights when the electricity goes out, and a variety of colors. Yes, I am ready to let there be light.

Lord, you know I do love candlelight—in church, in a fancy restaurant, at birthday parties, weddings, and even in spooky Halloween haunted houses. But today, I am thinking about my mother's old saying about some people who are so busy all the time they seem to be burning the candle at both ends.

If people were busy in my mother's day, they are even more hurried and harried today—burning the candle of life with great abandon. In our world, busy-ness has become the accepted way to live, as we all multitask and rush from place to place, chore to chore. We have lots of wonderful timesaving technology, but where does all that "saved" time go? Why does it seem that we never have enough time in any day.

Of course, Lord, we DO have enough time. We have all the time there is, all the time you gave us. But we have so many things to do, we have little time to be.

You notice, Lord, that I'm saying we and they when me and I are the appropriate words. My candle burns brightly because I do have a lot of involvements and I love them all but I know I should learn to prioritize and say no when it is best for me.

You should be able to teach me that, Lord, since you so often say no when I ask you for something that would not be good for me. And I'm always glad you do. Teach me your prioritizing way, Lord, so I can light-en up my life.

Put Your Foot in It!

A sock. A white sock. A cotton sock, made from the cotton plants that flourish in God's good earth. A sock to keep your toes warm. A sock you could put a rock in to use as a weapon against an attacker. A sock you wouldn't want to put a pebble in since it would make your toes sore. But a sock that teaches a lesson?

Well, maybe. Probably everybody else but me already knew this, but I just learned that the word *discalced* means "barefoot" (or sock-less?). I had always heard of "discalced" monks and nuns, but I never took the time to find out that it meant barefoot. Today most discalced orders wear sandals instead of going barefoot. And I bet maybe sometimes they might even wear socks with their sandals.

So there you are! I know that the good monks and nuns try to follow in the footsteps of Jesus— and I know I should too—and that's a good lesson for today.

OK, Lord, I know that's reaching a bit. But the next time I go barefoot in the grass or lounge shoeless at the pool, I'm going to tell everyone I am discalced—and see if they are as late as I was in learning what that means. And Lord, whether shod or unshod, I do want to follow in your footsteps. I know that won't be easy and I don't have a good track record so far. Too often I have put my foot into it. But I will try to be more careful and watch where I step—now that I have this sock lesson to remind me.

On the Ball...

This little ballpoint pen has sure been a good friend. It's there when I need it to jot down a grocery list, write a check, send a note to someone, address a get-well card—or write notes to myself!

Oh, yes, I need those ballpoint notes so I can keep on the ball. If it wasn't for the notes, I would probably forget to "Pick up Gloria by 7:45" so we will get to the meeting on time or "Put mail out before the mailman comes at 11 o'clock" so the checks will get delivered by the due date or "Plant the tulip bulbs today" since the weather is supposed to turn bad tomorrow. What would I do without my ballpoint?

Lord, I know that I should probably be writing more notes that say "save time to read the Bible TODAY" or "call your friend who recently lost her husband" or "take some flowers to that lady you don't like" (because she's sick and she doesn't know I don't like her so she might even be glad to see me).

However, Lord, you've probably noticed that I never need a note to remind me to bother YOU with all my whines and whimpers. Do you get tired of your cell phone ringing so often with my urgent messages? Sorry about that. But you must admit that I also call with yippees and hurrays about all the fantasmagorical blessings you are always sending my way. My diet, housekeeping, and checkbook may be unbalanced, but I do try to keep my prayer life balanced with equal amounts of frantic calls for help and grateful calls of thanks and praise.

But about that pen, Lord. I do want to thank you especially that we have advanced from those handmade feather pens my ancestors had to use and those ink-spilling pens that had to be filled by sucking up ink from a bottle. Even though amazing documents were drawn up and signed with feathers and wonderful books were written by those ink-spillers, I am truly grateful for my non-smudging, non-spilling ballpoint.

Sadly, ballpoint-signed documents preserved under glass may not look as impressive in museums but for day-to-day writing, this friendly little pen really helps keep me on the ball.

Through a (Magnifying) Glass Brightly

Wow! Things sure do seem different when you take time to look at them very closely. Who knew that little bug had six legs and weird wings? Who knew that tiny white thing wasn't part of the carpet design but a bit of cracker crumb the vacuum missed! Who knew my thumb fingerprint looked so different from the print God put on my next finger?

Well, Lord, this magnifying glass sure teaches lots of lessons. First, things are not always what they seem from a distance. Next, some things are much more interesting—and maybe more important—than you might notice if you don't take time to look closely. Also, checking the fine print on a label might be a good idea since that turns out to be the instructions—and if you read the instructions first instead of as a last resort, you can save lots of time.

Lord, Lord, I could learn so much if I would notice before I nag, and pray before I panic. Thank you so much for giving me this marvelous magnifying glass that might help me turn my small narrow picture into the wider view of your big picture. Too often I magnify the little silly problems of every day, wasting time worrying or talking about them instead of using that time to try to work out solutions. Then I fail to magnify the things that are important to you—and should be to me.

Lord, thank you for all the amazing things you put into this world that we can only discover by looking through a magnifying glass. But, Lord, I am so grateful you didn't decide to give us all magnifying eyes so that everyone could notice the cracker crumb in my carpet, the jelly fingerprint on the refrigerator door, or the bad mood sometimes hiding under my Monday morning smile. Thank you, Lord, thank you.

Nickel, Pickle, Tickle Me

What good is a nickel? It can't buy very much today. And I hardly notice it in my pocketful of change. But just look at it. It has designs on it that have changed through the years. There was once a buffalo and then a picture of Thomas Jefferson and his home known as Monticello and now the strange-looking ship that was used by Lewis and Clark as they sailed off to map the Louisiana Purchase. The nickel is a history lesson!

But there's more. Today I learned that between the years 1883 and 1912, the nickel was plated in 24k gold—and it was known as a Racketeer Nickel! That's because at that time, there was also a $5 gold coin that looked similar to the nickel, so crooks would often try to "pass" the five-cent gold coin for the five-dollar one. Today it tickled me to think of a crook getting caught and being in a pickle for nickel-passing!

Yes, Lord, I know it doesn't take much to tickle me. But that's OK. Thanks for giving me a silly sense of humor so I can usually find some silly something to tickle me out of a blue mood.

But back to that nickel, Lord. I also notice it is round, unending—like eternity, like the circle of life. So I am going to give the nickel more respect from now on. And every time I finger one when buying a burger or feeding a parking meter, I will try to remember to thank you for giving me this pocket history lesson plus a reminder of your priceless gift of eternity.

I Care Enough to Send the Very Cheapest

When you go to a card store, there are racks and racks of amazing greeting cards. Some are sooo funny. Some are sooo pretty. But some are also sooo expensive—sometimes too expensive to fit into a budget. But that's OK since I have an imagination and words and thoughts and pen and paper that I can use instead of dollars.

Actually, when I think about it, some of my most favorite greetings came written in crayon on construction paper!

Dear Lord, I guess I don't need to try to impress anyone with a big fancy card when maybe a short handwritten note would mean as much or more. But, Lord, maybe that's not enough. Maybe I should send a note AND a card and maybe a real rose or a real bouquet or...

OK, Lord, I'm overdoing it again. I'm always afraid it won't be enough, thinking I should do something extra special, something clever or amazing or just more than before. Teach me, Lord, to be generous but prudent, sincere but not intrusive, thoughtful but not going to extremes.

And, Lord, I guess maybe I sometimes do the same when I approach you. I think I haven't done enough good deeds or said enough prayers or accomplished enough great things to earn your approval. Remind me again, Lord, of the words of the Indian philosopher, Tagore, who said, "God waits for his temple to be built of love while his people bring stones." I do love you, Lord, so please help me to stop counting the stones.

Small Potatoes

I love these little "new" potatoes. They look like fun food. They don't look impressive or important and they're kinda lumpy instead of being perfectly round and they usually have little "dimples" in them. But maybe the dimples mean they are smiling because they know potatoes—even small potatoes—are important since they are a food favorite of people all over the world. When anyone thinks of a hot hearty family meal, they usually think of "meat and potatoes."

And when I think of potatoes, I always remember the time my inventive mother decided to use food coloring to tint the mashed potatoes pink. Then she pushed them through a pastry tube to put pink rose-shaped potatoes on our dinner plates.

For years, I thought she was the only one silly enough to stage food frights, but then I heard of a lady who wanted to do something colorful so she served a meal of brown roast beef, green beans, and pink mashed potatoes. When she noticed her husband and sons were eating the meat and beans very fast, she asked "What about the potatoes?" They said, "Potatoes? We were eating so fast because we wanted to get to the pink ice cream before it melted."

Dear Lord, thanks for all our crazy family memories. And thanks for potatoes, great and small. Only you could come up with a vegetable that has to be dug out of the ground and comes out caked with mud, all brown and ugly, but can be cooked into something so delicious, it's loved by folks, great and small, all over the world.

And, Lord, thank you for people who may not seem impressive or important and may be kinda ugly or lumpy and may or may not have dimples and may have to be dug out of their shyness or privateness—but turn out to be so delicious, they become treasured best friends.

Thank you, Lord, for teaching us to not judge too quickly, to dig more deeply and to treasure and enjoy your small potatoes.

The Ruling Class

I love this old ruler. I've had it for ages. When I look at it, I remember how it has helped me measure where to hang all those family photos on the hall wall, measure whether the kitchen door is wide enough to drag in a garage-sale treasure, and measure every corner and cranny of the house as I plot and plan and "rearrange" my worldly belongings. When I look at this ruler, it also reminds me that I will never be a member of the ruling class! But it SHOULD remind me that I better measure my steps and be more careful to follow some rules.

Yes, Lord, even this little ruler gives me pause for thought. Most of my life, others have seen me as a member of the goodie-two-shoes group rather than the double-dog-darers. Little did they know how good I am at "tweaking" some rules until I can manage to abide by them. Oh, I don't mean I've been secretly plotting jewel thefts or drawing up a list of best ways to eliminate a neighbor's barking dog. It's just that I sometimes fudge a bit here and there.

Lord, you know that when the truth hurts, I sometimes mumble around finding excuses for myself instead of fessing up and taking my earned dosage of medicine. When I'm late for an appointment, I might kinda hint that the traffic was just terrible when it wasn't. When I forget to do something, I might kinda hint that I was just so so busy that I couldn't fit it in my schedule instead of admitting it slipped my feeble mind. A goodie-two-shoes would never be so devious.

Sorry, Lord. You know I try to follow your big Top Ten rules known as commandments but some of those little daily ones do bring out the tweak in me. Please let this ruler teach me to measure up more and tweak less.

Open Sesame!

Ah, the little chain that holds the keys to my kingdom—the car key and the house keys. This is one of my most important possessions since it is the "open sesame" to my everyday life—yet it taunts me. It's here one minute, gone the next. No matter how careful I try to be to remember to leave the key chain on the peg by the kitchen door, some days it just isn't there! I look all over the house and finally, after a few moments of panic, I always manage to find that sneaky but valuable key chain.

But there's another kind of key that's not that easy to find—the key to the so-called inner me.

Dear Lord, you know that sometimes I take that key and lock myself away, refusing to open up when I should. Maybe I fail to see someone else's pain because I'm too focused on my own. Maybe I'm too busy doing "things" to notice that someone needs me to stop and give them my undivided attention. Maybe I'm spending too much time reading the newspaper when I should be trying to read the distress signals that are all around.

Help me find the "open sesame," Lord. Show me how to open up to the needs of others and still be able to close the door when it's necessary to save enough time to feed my soul, to smell the flowers, to rest, refresh and welcome peace.

Keys are wonderful, Lord, but it's sometimes hard to find them and even harder to know when and how to use them properly. Teach me the secret, Lord, to finding the keys to YOUR kingdom.

Which Animal Are You?

The other day a child asked me, "If you could be any kind of an animal, which one would you choose to be?" I really had to think about that. Not a hippopotamus—hippy is not my favorite nickname. Not a tiger or lion or even a cheetah—wild, fast jungle life may sound exciting but having to catch your food and eat it raw is not my idea of gourmet. No, I think I have the answer by looking at my little letter opener that has a cute kitty cat design perched on the end of it. Maybe choosing a kitty cat is a boring, obvious choice but that's my answer.

However, this brings up another question. Would I want to be a stay-in-the-house cat where I would be safe and petted and fed regularly, but would never be allowed out in the wide, wonderful world? Or would I choose to be a cat who was allowed in the house but let out each day to wander and explore, to meet the neighbors or hide in the bushes for some quiet time? That sounds good to me—but wait, that could be dangerous. I could get hit by a car or attacked by a big dog or I could snack on a plant that looked delicious but was really poisonous.

Well, Lord, you see that even imagining a

different lifestyle has its problems. Some days it's easy to think that any other lifestyle than mine might be more fun or less painful. I might want to become a mountain climber or a rock musician or the president of a small country or a beach bum—but they all have that risk element. I could fall or lose my hearing or get assassinated or get serious sunburn. Oh well, you didn't really design me to be physically or emotionally able to handle any of those jobs. But some days I think you didn't design me to handle the job I have. Yes, Lord, I know. Your design was OK. It's what I'm doing with it that is sometimes less than it could be.

So thank you, Lord, for not making me a hippo or a lion, a climber or a president—nor even a cat. Thank you for designing me so I can still imagine and wonder what if, for giving me a safe place to live but the freedom to explore, for helping me face the risks and enjoy the adventures. And thank you, Lord, for making children who challenge grownups to stay alert by endlessly asking questions.

Orange You Ready Yet?

Mmmm...this orange smells good and it looks bright like sunshine. But there is one problem with an orange—you can hardly find any word that will rhyme with it!

Well, oranges may not be good for making poems, but they are good for making orange juice, orange cake, orange sherbet, and orange marmalade. So, thank you, Lord, for making such a bright delicious rhymeless fruit.

You know, Lord, my grandma told me that she thought of oranges as a golden special treat. That's because when she was a little girl she never got an orange except at Christmastime— and then it was one orange in the toe of her Christmas stocking. When I was a little girl, I thought of an orange as a non-treat, way too sour for my delicate taste buds. My mother solved that by peeling an orange, slicing it very thin into pretty circles and sprinkling the golden circles with lots of sugar. As I happily slurped this sugary new treat, my mother could have said, "Now orange you sorry you misjudged this delicious fruit?" But she didn't.

Lord, have you noticed that I sometimes judge people and chores the way I did an orange? I meet a person and turn away because he or she seems too loud or too opinionated or wears weird clothes or has a really irritating voice. I look at a chore and judge it too messy, too hard, too time-consuming, or too trifling for my delicate work buds. The next time I do that, I better think about the orange and remember my mother's Mary Poppins recipe for most things in life—"a spoonful of sugar makes the medicine go down."

Lord, teach me to take a second look and consider a spoonful of compassion or tolerance, grit or elbow grease, before I judge people or jobs to be done. And please, Lord, don't say, "Orange you sorry it takes you so long to learn a lesson?"

A Sweeping Statement

This mini-feather duster is small enough to fit into a paper bag, but that's OK. It does a big job very well, frantically dusting off the most-seen spaces quickly when company is coming. It fits right in with a philosophy I adapted when I saw a small sign that read, "My idea of cleaning house is to sweep the room with a glance."

I admit it. I will never be chosen housecleaner of the universe. Through the years, I have tried to trick everyone into thinking my house is in order by making it look charmingly (and deceptively) well-kept because of all the house plants that hide the dust in the corners and the low-wattage lights that keep visibility to a minimum.

Well, Lord, as you know, my house and my life could use a good sweeping out. The surface may look OK but oh, those dust-balls are lurking. And I'm afraid, Lord, that I sometimes work like the feather duster, sweeping across the surface. Sometimes it works—but maybe it shouldn't.

I think of this when I go to the monthly Book Discussion Club. We have all read the same book. I have loved it or hated it, judged the writing, the title, and the message and am ready to toss my opinions in the pot. After I sound off, others in the group quietly point out little nuances that had sailed right past me. Some compare the book's style or message to other books they have read, books that were never on my reading list. Their comments always seem so much deeper than mine.

Lord, am I doing this spiritually too? Do I skim the surface when I should be delving deeper? Am I just naturally a shallow person or is there still hope for me? Maybe it's OK for me to be shallow when I'm reading an ordinary book, but I know I should delve more deeply when I'm reading your book or judging others or tossing my opinions in the pot. Thank you, Lord, for letting me be a feather duster sometimes, but help me know when it's important to do more than sweep a problem or a person with a glance.

Where's My Place?

When you like to read a lot or use reference books a lot, you need a lot of bookmarks —and I have a lot. Some are fancy and some are not, but they all know how to do a good job. And I am thinking today that this bookmark knows more than I do; it knows where my place is!

I put a book down, go away, and sometimes don't get back to that book for days or weeks—but when I do, the bookmark is still there so I know where my place is. In the same way, sometimes I go to a movie or a meeting with a friend and I say, "Save my place," then dash off to get popcorn or a program and when I come back, I know where my place is.

Lord, it's not that easy in the rest of life. Sometimes I'm not sure just where my place is. Sometimes I neglect a friendship or an opportunity or a responsibility and when I get back to it, things have changed. My "place" has not always been saved.

To a Special Teacher

"Study to show thyself approved unto God, a workman that needeth not to be ashamed, rightly dividing the word of truth."
II TIM 2:15

God Bless You

And sometimes, Lord, I am just the opposite of neglectful. I stick my nose in where it does not belong or speak up when I should keep quiet and make it obvious to all that I "do not know when to stay in my proper place."

Well, Lord, you've seen me do all those things wrong but no matter how many times I am too forward or too backward, too neglectful or too nosy, too ignorant to know where my place is, you always forgive me and give me a second chance.

I hope this means, Lord, that when I stumble down the backstretch of my life, you will still be there to let me know you have "saved my place."

Cut It Out!

These little snub-nose scissors are great and safe for the kids, but they are just one of the cutting-edge tools in my house. There are the kitchen scissors that are handy to cut some things for salad like cooked chicken or green onions. There are the scissors by my "reading" spot, handy to clip articles to save, oddities for my trivia file or grocery coupons. But my favorites are my mother's scissors.

Unlike me, my mother was a fabulous seamstress and I remember her using those scissors to cut out fabric for a new dress or a fancy evening gown or maybe just to shorten a hem. I use them now to cut off the sale tags from my store-bought bargain outfits!

Oh well, Lord, I didn't follow in my mother's footsteps when it came to sewing, but I still remember the lessons she taught about cutting out the bad things in life, cutting up to have fun, and sometimes using a slightly cutting remark to remind me that if I would only start a few minutes early I wouldn't always be a few minutes late.

Lord, there are a few cutting remarks in your book too—about "shalt nots." And you taught a lot of lessons in parables about cutting out the bad things in life. But I don't remember you dwelling much on cutting up for fun. Was that an oversight or did you think you didn't need to mention it because it was so obvious since you had made so many funny things for us to laugh about? Surely you wanted us to enjoy the silly antics of puppies and kittens, the strange necks of tall giraffes and hide-in-the-shell turtles, and all the giggly, gangly little kids who DO say the funniest things.

Lord, you know that even doctors say now that laughter is the best medicine so I hope you also laugh when you see your children cutting up to have fun. And, Lord, I sure hope that you don't mind and might even smile when someone has the audacity to make up silly prayers about things like potatoes and postage stamps, safety pins and scissors.